BATSFORD'S HERITAGE GUIDES

Shakespeare's
London

Malcolm Day

BATSFORD

Elizabethan London

When William Shakespeare, the young bard from Stratford, arrived in London in the late 1580s, he could hardly have imagined the contrast with the simple village life he was leaving behind. He found a city of magnificence and of squalor, and one of the world's most vibrant trade centres. This was the capital of probably the most adventurous nation in the world, which sent out explorers to all corners of the globe. Every day, tall ships would land at the docks to unload foreign merchandise and load the coffers of prosperous capitalists.

▸ Bust of Shakespeare at the Guildhall Gallery, London

William Shakespeare: A brief life

1564	Born in Stratford-upon-Avon, the third child of eight
1582	Marries Anne Hathaway
1583–5	Has a daughter, Susanna, and twins, Hamnet (dies aged 11) and Judith
Late 1580s	Comes to London and works as an actor at The Theatre, Shoreditch
From 1590	Works as playwright as well as actor
1599	Opens the Globe Theatre in Southwark
1603	On the accession of James I, his company receives royal patronage and they change name to The King's Men
1608	Shakespeare and the King's Men start performing at Blackfriars Theatre
1609	Sonnets (154) are published
1613	The Globe burns down. Shakespeare retires to Stratford
1616	Dies on 23 April

Map of London, 1572

The citizens of London

Business boomed in London in the second half of the sixteenth century, and its reputation in foreign countries was well established. The capital became a magnet for fortune-seekers both from the English provinces and from abroad. Every day, more immigrants piled into this already crowded habitat, and threatened to tip the metropolis into ungovernable chaos. By the close of the century, Elizabethan London had almost 200,000 inhabitants. Yet only 50 years earlier, the city had been just a quarter of this size.

Squeezing along twisting alleyways, a motley crowd rubbed shoulders: hawkers, milkmaids, blacksmiths, chimney sweeps, oyster-catchers, sailors, painted ladies, gentlemen in their finery and of course pickpockets, all making up a rich tapestry of humanity. Alongside them dawdled ducks, pigs and sheep soon to be slaughtered; stray cats and dogs would scatter before passing carts or carriages. Where, you might wonder, would everyone live in such a scrum?

Housing

As the City of London was bounded by Roman walls, there was no space to expand outwards, so just as today, house-owners built upwards. One tenement floor after another was added, each jutting out further over the street – like an inverted pyramid. In some of the higher-rise buildings, a tenant could lean out of a top floor window and almost touch the house opposite.

The crush within this still medieval infrastructure was fraught with problems, not least hygiene and the fear of plague. The light was poor, the air stale. Houses had no plumbing. Chamber pots were tipped directly on to the street. Drains had little chance of coping with the constant flush of domestic waste; a stream called Fleet Ditch, which ran through the city, was an open sewer and had a permanent stench. Except for scavenging birds and dogs, only rainfall served as an agent of sanitation, washing all the scum and dirt down into the River Thames.

A Tudor house in Tower Hill, from an engraving of 1793

Shakespeare's arrival in London

Any stranger arriving in such a mêlée would struggle, you might think, to find his feet. How did Shakespeare cope? Where did he live? Luckily, Shakespeare could turn to an old schoolfriend from Stratford, Richard Field. Like Shakespeare, Field had received a classical grammar-school education, which in those days was highly academic – schoolboys had to be able to converse with each other in Latin.

By the time Shakespeare came to London, Field had established himself as a translator and publisher. It is likely that he found lodgings for his old school chum near to his own rooms in Blackfriars. Being a publisher, it is also likely that Field introduced his friend to the poets and playwrights of the time, for the literary world was a small one – everyone knew everyone else. Their friendship was close enough for Shakespeare to use his name in *Cymbeline*, rendered as 'Richard du Champ', or Richard Field. And it was Field who published Shakespeare's poems *Venus and Adonis* and *The Rape of Lucrece*.

River Thames

This great river, upon which the Romans had created the city of Londinium, was at once the capital's sewer and its lifeblood. Up the Thames estuary came food and luxurious bounty: fine silks, gold, silver and exotica from the East; out went finely worked oak and garments produced by the wool mills. As well as being used for overseas trade, the river was a concourse for London's inhabitants. London Bridge was the only means of crossing the river on foot, and the best way to get about was often by boat. Hired rowing boats would ferry passengers upstream and downstream, from one bank to the other. Close your eyes and imagine the lapping river, clinking of oars and boatmen's chatter – a scene reminiscent of modern Venice.

▼ Old London Bridge, 1597

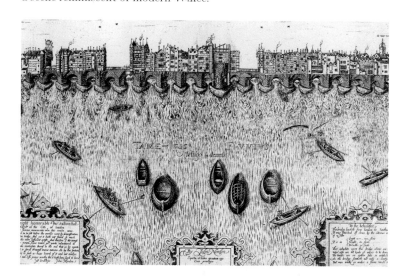

London: an inspiration?

No doubt Shakespeare did, at times, just let the sights and sounds of London drift through his mind. For this was what the playwright drew upon for inspiration. The contrast between the urban and the rural life of his upbringing, the divisions between rich and poor, the tensions wrought by such a complex society – which as an outsider he was able to observe with detachment – were all grist to his creative mill. Although his plays are often set in foreign lands, it was here among the alleyways and taverns, the seedy brothels and elegant mansions that Shakespeare found the material for his tragedies and comedies. The characters of his invention dwelt among those he saw every day about him, and those with whom he was acquainted – his friends and enemies.

◄ The galleried
George Inn,
Southwark

Shakespeare's plays

1590–1600	Shakespeare writes more than 20 history plays, including *Richard III*, *Henry V* and *Julius Caesar*, and romantic comedies, such as *The Taming of the Shrew*, *Love's Labour's Lost*, *A Midsummer Night's Dream*, *Much Ado About Nothing* and *Twelfth Night*
1600–1608	Shakespeare's major tragedies are written in this period, including *Hamlet*, *Othello*, *Macbeth* and *King Lear*, and 'dark' comedies, such as *Measure for Measure* and *All's Well That Ends Well*
1607–1611	Classical plays, including *Antony and Cleopatra* and *Coriolanus*

Total number of surviving plays = 38

Londoners, of course, made up Shakespeare's audiences, and were therefore his livelihood. Over the 20 or so years prior to Shakespeare's arrival in the late 1580s, the theatre had become something of a novelty. Though the Greeks performed theatrical drama in ancient times, the idea of a proper stage and auditorium was unknown to London folk. Impromptu sketches were put on in inn courtyards – one famous venue was John Brayne's Red Lion in Whitechapel – but actors were regarded by the law as no better than 'rogues, vagabonds and sturdy beggars'. That changed in the 1570s, when licensing was introduced. Overnight, acting became a respectable profession.

Shakespeare on theatre:
'The purpose of playing ... is to hold, as 'twere, the mirror up to nature; to show virtue her own feature ...'
Hamlet, *Hamlet*, Act 3, Scene 2

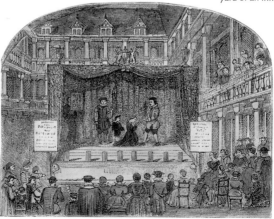

A play performed in the yard of an inn

The first theatres

Brayne and a fellow entrepreneur, James Burbage, decided to emulate the Ancient Greeks and in 1576 bought some land at Liberty of Holywell in Shoreditch, in the northern suburbs, where they opened London's first theatre. It consisted of a wooden, polygonal auditorium with galleries and an open stage, around which spectators would stand and watch, thrilled by the new plays. It was called simply The Theatre – and it was here that William Shakespeare made his first appearances as an actor.

Hamlet with the skull of Yorick

The venture was an immediate success, and very soon another playhouse, The Curtain, went up next door. It is perhaps no surprise that Shakespeare came to London when he did, as playgoing was becoming all the rage.

A quote that could easily have been a word of advice from Shakespeare to his fellow actors:

'Assume a virtue, if you have it not.'
Hamlet, *Hamlet*, Act 3, Scene 4

Map of Bankside
showing bull- and
bear-baiting pits

Theatre and sin outside the city walls

The Romans built a wall around Londinium in about AD 200, to defend the city. In Elizabethan times, London Wall was made up largely of the old Roman wall, with ten gates that allowed the populace in and out of the 'Square Mile', as the old city is still known today. The area was controlled by the lord mayor, who lived at the Mansion House. A tall watchtower, built in medieval times on the site of the present-day Barbican, loomed over the high stone wall to keep an eye out for any unwanted intruders.

Laws introduced to protect citizens included a ban on all drama, which was considered much too immoral to be allowed to foul the minds of the Christian faithful. Thus, the first theatres had to be erected outside the city walls, in Shoreditch (about 0.8 km [½ mile] away), and over the river at Bankside in Southwark. Outside the city walls was a netherworld of criminality and prostitution. Thieves, conmen and gamblers plied their trade and patronised bawdy taverns where harlots would entertain for a meagre living. Early theatrical productions in London were part of this scene.

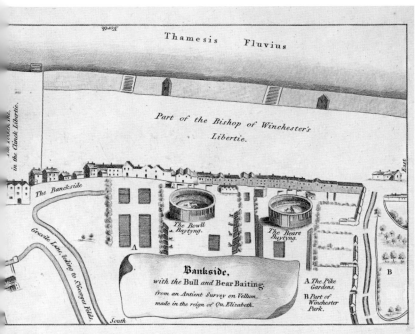

North

Thamesis Fluvius

Part of the Bishop of Winchester's Libertie.

The Bankside

Grevile Lane, leading to St Georges Fields

The Bowll Bayting.

The Beare Bayting.

A

B

South

Bankside,

with the Bull and Bear Baiting,

from an Antient Survey on Vellum,

made in the reign of Qu. Elizabeth.

A The Pike Gardens.

B Part of Winchester Park.

THE above curious PLAN of BANKSIDE

tate, not else...

...tends from the extremity of Winchester Park, to Old Paris Garden Lane,

riars Bridge)... ...t is the Falcon Inn, which, till of late

m whence co... ...o St Saviours, is now

communicat... ...iting, are represented

or keeping t... ...ed in the name of Pike,

idently, at th...

Pipes and ale for Elizabethans

13

The Lord Chamberlain's Men

Following his ambitious nose, Shakespeare was soon writing plays for The Theatre. By 1594 he was living in Bishopsgate and had joined a troupe known as the Lord Chamberlain's Men (named after the group's patron, the queen's chamberlain). This was a large company and gave him greater opportunities to progress. It was with them that he would have staged the first performances of his history plays, *Henry VI, Part I*, *Part II* and *Part III*, and *Richard III*. The latter deals with the beginning of the Tudor ruling dynasty; Elizabeth I, the monarch who reigned during much of Shakespeare's life, was the last member of this dynasty. At this time Shakespeare also wrote the magical-realist comedy, *A Midsummer Night's Dream*, and his famous tragedy, *Romeo and Juliet*, the tale of ill-fated lovers who endeavour to escape their feuding families.

Romeo and Juliet at their dawn parting

Life as an actor-writer

It is believed that the bard produced three other plays
in this period: *The Taming of the Shrew*, *Titus
Andronicus* and *Love's Labour's Lost*. For such a prolific
output, one would think he had plenty of time to dwell
on his plots and characters, honing them to perfection
without the demands of a busy day job. However, the
reality was quite the opposite.

As a full member of the theatre company, he would
have spent the mornings in rehearsal, the afternoons
performing, and the evenings handling stage business,
sometimes listening to new plays to be added to the
repertoire. He was also known to be a frequenter of
taverns, where no doubt his fellow thespians would have
tempted him to relax after work (though it is believed
that Shakespeare drank and indulged very little).
Precious little time remained for penning his
masterpieces, worked out perhaps in the early hours of
the morning by candlelight, dead with fatigue. It is
quite possible that he was working flat out just to earn
his keep, as records state that in 1597 he owed taxes
while living in the parish of St Helen's in Bishopsgate.

Shakespeare was but one of thousands to migrate to 'merry London', as it was known. Many came to make their names and to enjoy life while they were at it. Poets, playwrights, merchants and entrepreneurs settled along the banks of the Thames amid a great jumble of disparate buildings. With no planning restrictions, no zoning of commercial activities, landowners could build anything anywhere. One writer described the scene as: 'Here a palace, there a woodyard; here a garden, there a brewhouse; here dwelt a lord, there a dyer …'

And there was no shortage of funds poured into architectural fancy, creating a busy skyline of spires and pinnacles with eccentric features. Among the most admired were the church of St Mary-le-Bow, with elaborate lanterns on its steeple, and the grand Flemish façades of the Royal Exchange, with its fanciful bell column. How Shakespeare's day must have been punctuated by the peal of bells all around him.

London Bridge

London's only bridge was a trunk route linking north and south. It was similar in concept to the covered Ponte Vecchio, which survives in Florence. Fine houses and shops ran along its length. The bridge had 19 piers

Old London
Bridge in 1600

An Elizabethan
drinking party

to support the weight of the packed, grandiose edifices, and was one of the longest man-made spans of a river in the world. Such was the scale of commerce that took place upon the bridge that the royal surveyor described it as 'a little city … in itself'.

Of all the elegant buildings that graced the bridge, the finest must have been Nonsuch House. Its name literally meaning 'no other such house', the house was imported block by block from Holland, and stood in glorious colour, with ornate onion domes and characteristic Dutch carved gables, a monument to the extravagant gesturing of the age.

St Paul's Cathedral

Crowning all was the majestic St Paul's Cathedral, not yet with the dome we see today, and minus its steeple (which burned down in 1561). But its massive, transepted nave and central square tower loomed head and shoulders over the rest like an archbishop over his minions. In this turbulent age it seems that nowhere was sacred, for even this hallowed space became more than just a place of worship. The main aisle served as a thoroughfare for all and sundry, trudging up Ludgate Hill from Fleet Street; an informal meeting place to exchange ideas and chat.

Publishers purloined the cathedral yard for their bookstalls, where they sold the latest books. Most belonged to the Stationers' Company, which had been named after the earlier bookstalls at fixed positions around St Paul's and from which the word 'stationery' is derived. Half of Shakespeare's plays were sold here and one of the sellers would have been his old schoolfriend, Richard Field.

The importance of patronage

Books were expensive to produce. Even though they could now be printed relatively quickly using the revolutionary Caxton press, the price of binding, paper and ink all meant that an author's wages remained low. Writers depended on patronage for security. In general, it was the aristocracy who supported books and the writing of them. The illustrious patron of playwrights was William Herbert, 3rd Earl of Pembroke, who resided at Baynard's Castle, which overlooked the river a short way from St Bride's.

The metaphysical poet and preacher John Donne lodged in a large house in Drury Lane, provided by his patron Sir Robert Drury. During these comfortable years, the poet produced probably his best work. In St Paul's stands a marble effigy of Donne (1572–1631), the only monument in the cathedral to have survived the Great Fire of London in 1666.

Rivalry and duels

Writers needed patronage, and there was a good deal of competition for it. By 1592, Shakespeare had established a reputation for himself as an actor and playwright, an achievement that drew a mixed response. One jealous rival, Robert Greene, in penning a pamphlet, *A Groat's Worth of Wit*, dismissed him as an 'upstart crow' who plagiarized his better contemporaries. The struggle for primacy would often cause fellow actors and playwrights to clash.

The fact that many Elizabethan actors also engaged in fencing could make matters worse. A leading playwright of the day, Ben Jonson, argued with one rising star, challenged him to a duel and in the ensuing combat, killed the man. Jonson escaped hanging only by reading the 'neck verse', a loophole in the law enabling the well educated to earn reprieve by reading a verse from the Bible in Latin. One of the period's leading comic actors and a colleague of Shakespeare, Will Kemp, fell out with Shakespeare (whom he called 'Shakerags') over the role of the clown, a figure designed not merely to entertain but to get under the skin of an audience.

▲ Ben Jonson's plays
▶ Will Kemp

Taverns

Emerging writers would have met at taverns and batted ideas about over a tankard of ale. For playwrights, who needed good actors, sometimes at short notice (especially when plague took its toll), the tavern proved to be a useful recruiting ground. Some of the parts Shakespeare played would almost certainly have arisen here. He certainly worked a good deal with Ben Jonson, who was full of admiration for his witty contemporary. As he had considerable influence over his many followers, Jonson's compliments carried weight. When he adjudged Shakespeare's writing to plumb the depths of the human condition, Jonson did much to propel his ally on the road to success. After Shakespeare's death, Jonson described him as 'not of an age, but for all time'.

▶ Playwright Christopher Marlowe

Murder in a pub brawl

The tavern was a good source of material for Shakespeare's plays. The social environment and lifestyle of his companions would have helped forge characters of all sorts: gentlemen, thieves, conmen, comedians and the boisterous. Fuelled by flagons of liquor, tempers would rise and many an evening would end in a brawl. One infamous night in Deptford in 1593, a brawl involved England's best playwright of the time, Christopher Marlowe, author of *Tamburlaine the Great* and *Dr Faustus*.

Described by the poet Seamus Heaney (b. 1939) as a cross between Oscar Wilde and Jack the Ripper, Marlowe was perhaps always likely to come to a sticky end one day. Why he was spending the evening at the Eleanor Bull public house is unclear, though he may have been on the run. It is known that a quarrel developed with his drinking partners, and that Marlowe was stabbed above the eye with his own dagger after allegedly attacking one of them. He died on the spot, cursing.

It is quite possible that some skulduggery was involved, for Marlowe had become an enemy of the State for his outspoken atheism and blasphemy. The man who committed the murderous deed, Ingram Frizer, was one of a secret party of Elizabethan spies who may have been hired assassins. Marlowe's body is buried in the churchyard of St Nicholas's Church in Deptford.

The Globe Theatre

The final year of the sixteenth century witnessed a key development in Shakespeare's career. By then the company to which he belonged, the Lord Chamberlain's Men, had been going for five years – quite a feat when many troupes of the period were forming and just as quickly folding. The ensemble had produced about 100 plays in that time: nearly a quarter of them were Shakespeare's. His writing soared to new heights. In 1599 alone he finished *Henry V*, created *Julius Caesar* and *As You Like It*, and penned the first draft of *Hamlet*. It is no coincidence that this was also the year that the Globe Theatre, of which he became co-owner, was founded.

The Globe Theatre

New departures

The Lord Chamberlain's Men had been making the best
of a difficult situation in Shoreditch. The land upon
which The Theatre was built did not belong to them
and the lease had expired. The Lord Chamberlain's
Men, now led by the charismatic Richard Burbage (son
of the deceased James, founder of The Theatre) and
others, thought that Southwark, with its livelier
entertainments south of the river, would be a better
venue. But how to do it? Building a theatre was an
expensive business and this company, although doing
quite well, could not stretch to that. Necessity being
the mother of invention, a plot was hatched.

A furtive mission

In the dead of night over Christmas 1598, a grave band
of players gathered in Shoreditch armed with tools.
While the landlord was away at his home in Essex,
they set about their secret mission of repossessing what
they considered to be rightfully theirs: the building of
The Theatre itself. Post by post, they dismantled the
frame and loaded it on to horse-drawn wagons. A long,
thin convoy slowly crunched its way through the snow
of Bishopsgate to Peter Street, near Bridewell Stairs on
the waterfront. One story goes that the men crossed
the near-frozen river on foot, but such a venture would
have been a risk too far, even if the river was indeed
ice-bound. Instead, the timbers were stored in a
warehouse over winter until a venue in Southwark
was found.

A performance at the reconstructed Globe Theatre

The Globe goes up

The following spring, the company made a deal with a respected landlord who leased them a site on Bankside. The grand removal operation resumed; with the tolls of London Bridge being prohibitively expensive, the only option was to ferry the parts over the river. But with due diligence, come the summer of 1599, the Lord Chamberlain's Men had faithfully reassembled the former playhouse. Triumphantly, the new theatre was named the Globe, after its emblem showing the Greek god Atlas bearing the weight of the world.

The business was owned communally: Richard Burbage and his brother Cuthbert had one half-share, the other half was split between Shakespeare and four fellow players. The Globe was a striking building (you can see the reconstructed theatre today: it opened on the South Bank in 1997, 230 m [251 yd] from its original site off Park Street). The theatre was round, with tiered seats surrounding a projecting stage; the 'wooden O' mentioned in the Prologue to Shakespeare's *Henry V* – possibly the opening play – probably referred to its shape. (Certainly, in the light of the realm's triumphant defeat of the mighty Spanish Armada in 1588 and the renewed threat that summer, the patriotic tone of *Henry V* would have met with resounding approval from its proud nationalistic audience.) A window dedicated to Shakespeare now features in Southwark Cathedral.

> '... Can this cockpit hold the vasty fields of France? Or may we cram within this wooden O the very casques that did affright the air at Agincourt?'
> Narrator, *Henry V*, Prologue

Elizabethan theatre in the round at the Globe

Bankside: entertainment for the masses

The site chosen for the new playhouse was the Clink Liberty, so called because of the prisons in the district. One in three inhabitants of the district were watermen, who earned their living ferrying passengers across the river for a penny a ride. The Olde Swann (which has survived as Old Swan Stairs) was a common destination on the north bank for boats to moor up.

The district was certainly colourful. Unlike the artisan neighbourhood of his previous homestead, Shakespeare now had to lodge in an altogether rougher, more licentious environment. One contemporary writer described it as a 'continual alehouse'.

As well as bawdy inns, there were plenty of brothels, already two theatres, and arenas for bear- and bull-baiting, where crowds gawped and jeered at tethered bears, goaded to lash out at their mastiff assailants. There was no shortage of entertainment here for the masses. The area thus chosen to locate the Globe – where Shakespeare would stage his subtle art – was a sort of gross Elizabethan theme park, whose base level was blood-lust and sex.

Bear-baiting with mastiffs

◄ Artist's impression of an Elizabethan playhouse

▼ The new Globe on the South Bank

London Borough of Southwark

The
Rose Theatre
Built here in 1587
First
Elizabethan theatre
of Bankside

Voted by the People

▸ A blue plaque marks Bankside's first theatre

The Rose Theatre

Though drama on the stage was riding a wave of popularity, it still had to compete with such low forms of entertainment if it was to survive. The first theatre to be built on Bankside, in 1588, was the Rose, so named because it was once the site of a brothel (Rose being a common name among prostitutes). Its star impresario, Edward Alleyn, filled the auditorium with thrilling productions by Christopher Marlowe and Ben Jonson. But even this high-minded thespian hedged his bets by buying a share in the rival Bear Garden.

The success of Burbage's daring venture at the Globe was soon apparent for all to see, as audiences flocked to see exciting and hilarious new productions, especially those by William Shakespeare. As the new century turned, so the Rose was forced to close. Its company, the Lord Admiral's Men (named after Lord Howard, Admiral of the Fleet – the fleet that destroyed the Armada) moved premises across the river to outside Cripplegate, where they named their theatre the Fortune.

Shakespeare reading his work to Elizabeth I

The queen's man

As Shakespeare became the toast of the day, so he was invited increasingly to perform before the queen at the royal residence, Whitehall Palace, and at Richmond Palace. A bumbling character, Sir John Falstaff, from Shakespeare's play *Henry IV, Part I* and *Part II*, became a favourite among courtiers who would mockingly liken him to their real-life fellows. It is said that the queen too found Falstaff amusing and to ingratiate himself, Shakespeare found a part for this figure of fun in *The Merry Wives of Windsor*, which some think he wrote for Elizabeth. Whether or not this is true, the playwright included clear references to the queen in various plays, including *Henry V, Henry VIII* and, most romantically, in *A Midsummer Night's Dream*, as well as some of the sonnets. Shakespeare was clearly enamoured of the monarch and he was her favourite playwright.

Falstaff hides in laundry

Many of Shakespeare's plays are set overseas and involve court intrigues. One German visitor to London wryly noted that the English find out about foreign affairs by watching Shakespeare's plays. Though most Elizabethans would never have stepped beyond the shores of Britain, news of naval skirmishes with Spain, piracy, and the colourful tales of returning seamen made playgoers curious about all things from far-off lands. Furthermore, there was a big boom in foreign trade, reaching out to every corner of the globe, as enterprising merchants followed the imperial flag. In return, foreign traders were drawn to London, which, by the turn of the sixteenth century, had become perhaps the greatest entrepôt on earth.

Both sides of the River Thames east of London Bridge – being the furthest point upstream that ships could dock – were packed with wharves for unloading commodities. The buildings of Shakespeare's day have now been replaced by Victorian ones, but these stand as reminders of their original commercial purposes: Old Billingsgate Market (formerly Billingsgate fish market), for example, and Custom House on the north bank; while on Bankside there is Hay's Galleria, once the huge food wharf.

The heyday of big business

The brave new world of venture capitalism formed the background to Shakespeare's play *The Merchant of Venice*. All too familiar with the perils of risky undertakings, the shareholders of the new Globe were immersed in a commercial environment that constantly endeavoured to outstrip its rivals in the march of progress. Key symbols of this culture, such as the Royal Exchange, stood before them.

◄ Defeat of the Spanish Armada, 1588

The Merchant of Venice

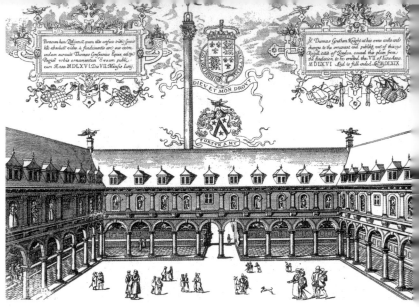

▲ The
Royal Exchange

► Thomas
Gresham's golden
grasshopper

The Royal Exchange

The Royal Exchange, erected in 1565 between Cornhill and Threadneedle Street, was a merchants' emporium designed with colonnaded loggias surrounding a piazza modelled on the bourses of Antwerp and Venice. Its founding entrepreneur, Sir Thomas Gresham, anticipated England's capital becoming a world leader, and his emblem of a grasshopper topping the bell column became a magnet to overseas traders.

The East India Company

One by one, other British businessmen followed Gresham's example. One of the most conspicuous enterprises was the East India Company, which was based in Leadenhall Street. Granted a royal charter in 1600 to trade in the Far East, the creation of this joint-stock organization enabled investors to share in the profits of trade voyages. From its flamboyant premises at East India House, it also conducted the long rule of colonial India (the building itself, on the site of the present Lloyds building, lasted until fire destroyed it in 1726).

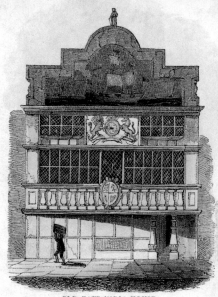

OLD EAST INDIA HOUSE.

Old East India House, before it was burnt down

Other Elizabethan charters included the Muscovite Company for deals with Russia, the Turkey Company, and the Hudson Bay Company for the Americas.

A few years after the death of Queen Elizabeth I in 1603, the New Exchange, a rival to the Royal Exchange, opened in the Strand. With its variety of small traders selling their wares on two floors, this became a prototype of the modern department store

The White Hart,
Bishopsgate

Multi-ethnic communities

With the free interchange of cross-channel cargo came the equally free flow of its operatives. Immigration was extensive and in Elizabethan times, London had become a multi-ethnic community. A strong Jewish community centred on Houndsditch at the end of Bishopsgate, one of the main gateways into the north of the City of London. New arrivals could be put up at two large hostelries, the Dolphin Inn and the White Hart, which stood just outside the gate. Also located here was Bethlem Royal Hospital (which became known as Bedlam), the infamous lunatic asylum, now the site of Liverpool Street Station. Locals made their livelihoods as pawnbrokers and market stallholders, selling second-hand clothes and suspect jewellery.

The city also housed several thousand black people, who made up a considerable minority of often highly valued workers. Some were servants, but there were also musicians, dancers and other entertainers.

'... I am a Jew. Hath not a Jew eyes? Hath not a Jew hands, organs, dimensions, senses, affections, passions; fed with the same food, hurt with the same weapons, subject to the same diseases, heal'd by the same means, warm'd and cool'd by the same winter and summer, as a Christian is?

Shylock, *The Merchant of Venice*, **Act 3, Scene 1**

Pirates and slaves

The number of black immigrants in the capital swelled as more slaves were freed from captured Spanish galleons. The British government's endorsement of pirate activity in the West Indies, involving the looting of Spanish treasure, was part of a policy to limit the growing wealth of the Spanish crown in the hope that by so doing, they would restrict Spain's ability to build a navy strong enough to invade England.

But as the streets of London filled with maimed veterans of the Irish rebellion begging for survival, rises in immigration put local communities under increasing pressure. A curiosity hitherto about all things exotic and unfamiliar began to turn to fear. The situation came to a head in 1601, when prejudice fuelled ill feeling and prompted a government edict officially labelling the black community 'a nuisance'. There were even suggestions that all blacks should be deported.

Othello and the sleeping Desdemona

Embassy from Morocco

Amid the gathering social and political turmoil, an official deputation from Morocco arrived in London in 1600. The short visit may have provided Shakespeare with the inspiration for *Othello*, his tragedy dealing with themes of jealousy and murder. The title role is that of a Moor in the Venetian army, who is driven into a jealous rage against his wife Desdemona by the scheming Iago.

It is no wonder that Shakespeare wrote so many plays about court intrigue and murder. The late Elizabethan age was riddled with conspiracies – and conspiracy theories. In fact, the crown was so paranoid that even Sir Walter Raleigh was accused of scheming against the queen. One plot after another was ruthlessly exposed by an extensive secret service. The spymaster, Sir Francis Walsingham, secretary of the Privy Council (chief officers of state), is said to have had more than 50 agents working for him in foreign courts. Shakespeare's classic line, on the lips of Julius Caesar, 'Et tu, Brute?' (Even you, Brutus?) has come to epitomise the ultimate betrayal by a close friend.

Catholic conspiracies

Plots were often complex and treacherous, involving various motives. Catholic Spain made use of disenfranchised Catholics, many of whom fled England when Mass was outlawed. One such refugee, Edmund Campion, son of a London bookseller, courageously re-entered the country in disguise and tried to spread the Catholic manifesto. Alas, he was found out and faced the standard penalty for treason: torture by rack in the Tower of London, followed by trial in Westminster Hall and the inevitable sentence to death by hanging.

Sir Francis Walsingham

Stuart dynasty

Sir Francis Walsingham was never defeated: no monarch was assassinated in his time. In 1603 Queen Elizabeth I died of natural causes after a 45-year reign and was mourned by her subjects for months, fondly remembered as 'Good Queen Bess'. Thus ended the Tudor dynasty and began the Stuart – or Jacobean – line. Her successor, King James I – also James VI of Scotland, thus uniting the two kingdoms – heralded a new period of security for Shakespeare and his acting troupe.

James I feasting with Spanish ambassadors

Royal dynasties

The Tudors began with Henry VII (1485–1509) and included his successor Henry VIII (1509–47). The dynasty also included Elizabeth I (1558–1603), but because her reign was long and many developments occurred, the period carries its own definition, 'Elizabethan'.

The Stuarts began with James I (1603–25) and continued to Queen Anne (1702–14), with a hiatus during the Interregnum (1649–1660), when Oliver Cromwell led the country as a republic. The period known as Jacobean relates to the reign of James I and mostly refers to styles of architecture and drama developed during his reign.

The coronation procession of Elizabeth I in 1558

A new name

The new king honoured Shakespeare's troupe with the title 'Grooms of the Chamber'. This made them members of the royal household and as such, they fell under the king's patronage with a licence to perform in the City of London. In honour of this change in their fortunes, the players upgraded their name from the Lord Chamberlain's Men to the King's Men.

As a mark of his new status, each 'groom' received enough scarlet cloth from the Royal Wardrobe in Blackfriars to make a suit. Thus attired, the players would take part in state occasions, giving performances for the king and his guests. One distinct advantage of such a position was that no member could ever be charged with indebtedness.

The arrest of Guy Fawkes

The Gunpowder Plot

The most famous of all the plotters were a coterie of Irish Catholics. On 5 November 1605, a conspiracy to bomb the state opening of Parliament by King James I was suspected. Walsingham's henchmen discovered one of the conspirators, Guy Fawkes, guarding 20 barrels of gunpowder hidden in a vault beneath the Houses of Parliament. He had no choice but to admit his intention and was led away to face the same fate as Edmund Campion.

Jacobean drama

In the Stuart era, drama in general became more intense, more passionate and more violent than that of the Elizabethan era. In tune with this, Shakespeare's writing in this period shows greater emphasis on tragedy, corruption and human weakness. Those plays considered to be among the best of his serious works were created between 1603 and 1606: *Othello*, *King Lear* and *Macbeth*. As with *Hamlet*, the theme of revenge takes centre stage in all these plays. *King Lear* dramatizes the tragic effects of the king's misjudgement of his children; and *Macbeth* deals with ambition and supernatural toying with the desire for power.

Well-known contemporaries of Shakespeare in the Jacobean period include Beaumont and Fletcher, Ben Jonson and John Webster. The latter wrote *The White Devil* and *The Duchess of Malfi*, plays about tragic heroines that reflect the social problems of the time, in which women suffer as victims of male violence.

Macbeth dons his
Scottish crown

Bubonic plague

Of course the noblest of human ideals could never deflect the great leveller of the age: the plague. Intermittently, Londoners suffered outbreaks of this highly contagious disease. There was no cure. In 1603 a devastating epidemic hit the city. Starting in the outlying districts, the disease spread through London, killing some 30,000 inhabitants within the year. Its toll was not equalled until the Great Plague of 1665. The worst bouts forced theatres to close temporarily and during these spells, Shakespeare retreated to his garret to write poetry – the royal patronage paying for his keep.

Shakespeare's sonnets

A collection of poems written by Shakespeare followed the form, invented in Italy, known as the sonnet. A sonnet was constructed of three stanzas, each with four lines, and ended with a rhyming couplet (two lines). The theme was nearly always love.

SHAKE-SPEARES

S O N N E T S.

Neuer before Imprinted.

AT LONDON
By *G. Eld* for *T. T.* and are
to be folde by *John Wright, dwelling*
at *Chrift Church gate.*
1609.

Title-page of the "Sonnets, 1609

Shakespeare wrote his sonnets in the 1590s, when the plague forced theatres to close. As well as having a particular form, the sonnets tend to be written in sequence, continuing a theme. The first 126 sonnets were addressed to a young man of fine physical and intellectual attributes, urging him to lead a virtuous life. Most of the rest are addressed to a mysterious 'dark lady', whose sensuous beauty and doubtful morals obsess the author. Themes of illicit liaisons and fateful consequences are among those expressed in beautiful language that gave his contemporaries a foretaste of the great tragedies he would write; *Hamlet, Macbeth, King Lear, Othello* and *The Tempest*.

While Shakespeare and his troupe were putting on plays, first at The Theatre in Shoreditch and then at the Globe, a further site had been obtained with a view to creating London's first indoor theatre. In 1596, James Burbage spent the sum of £600 on an old Dominican priory, which he intended to convert. The property had been requisitioned by Henry VIII during the Dissolution of the Monasteries, and had since fallen into disuse. Its name was Blackfriars, after the robes worn by the monks. (The site is at Playhouse Yard, Blackfriars.)

Children's theatre

However, once Burbage had converted the premises into a playhouse, well-to-do local residents objected to the idea of rowdiness in the neighbourhood, and performances were banned. Instead, Burbage leased the premises to children's companies. In 1597 Richard Burbage, James's son, inherited the theatre. He leased it to a lawyer, Henry Evans, who managed to obtain a warrant to set up a youth theatre group, called Paul's Children, drawn from local choirs and grammar schools, with the aim of providing entertainment for Queen Elizabeth I.

Avant-garde

From this beginning, the theatre prospered as new young writers produced plays. As time went on, it gradually developed a reputation for ground-breaking Jacobean drama. These new plays, challenging the boundaries of traditional satire, drew more sophisticated audiences than the theatres on Bankside. Although Blackfriars had a much smaller auditorium, its clientele was of a higher class and could be charged a good deal more for the seats. The very cheapest seat at Blackfriars, costing sixpence, was the same price as the most expensive seat at the Globe. Furthermore, these high prices tended to exclude the more boisterous elements of the hoi polloi, ensuring that an appropriate atmosphere could be maintained.

The theatre also introduced technical innovations, such as artificial lighting, of which the open-air theatres on Bankside naturally had no such need. From the stage directions that Shakespeare supplied on the script of *The Tempest*, it seems he had the new features of this theatre in mind for its performance.

The King's Men take over

The theatre did so well that in 1608 the King's Men, the troupe led by Richard Burbage, which now had a much sounder financial base under royal patronage, took back possession. The Burbage brothers, Richard and Cuthbert, remained as owners and shares were divided equally among several players of the company, including Shakespeare,

The Black Friar pub in Blackfriars

and the manager, Henry Evans. Running this venue as well as the Globe brought a huge increase in revenue for the King's Men. The company could now perform over the winter months on the indoor stage at Blackfriars, and spend the summer at the Globe. With seat prices at Blackfriars costing up to two shillings and sixpence, the revenue from this theatre proved considerably greater than from the Globe.

Shakespeare buys a house

Shakespeare's stock was certainly rising. One public record shows that at last he was able to buy a house. In 1613 he purchased 'Blackfriars Gatehouse', situated some 182 m (200 yd) behind the theatre, attached to what is now called Ireland Yard. When Shakespeare died three years later, his daughter inherited the house.

William's brother Edmund, also an actor, had lodged in Maid Lane some years earlier. He died in 1607 and was buried in the churchyard of what was then St Saviour's Church, and is now Southwark Cathedral.

The Globe in flames

The newfound wealth of the King's Men allowed them to overcome a major setback in 1613, when the Globe burned down. The company's resources were such that they could afford to rebuild it, this time with a tiled roof rather than the highly combustible thatch that had covered the first model. They also had to replace costumes and stage sets that were lost in the flames Fortunately, the company held duplicates of their scripts at Blackfriars. Such an outcome was not the case for the Admiral's Men, who lost everything when their Fortune Theatre burned down in 1621.

Places to Visit

Shakespeare's Globe [1 on map overleaf]
21 New Globe Walk, London SE1 9DT (www.shakespeares-globe.org)
Reconstruction of the octagonal theatre Shakespeare part-owned
with his company The Chamberlain's Men. See picture below.

Rose Theatre [2]
Bankside, London (www.rosetheatre.org.uk)
Excavations in 1989 near the Globe Theatre revealed a large
amount of the site of the original Elizabethan theatre, the first to
be built in Southwark. From a viewing platform visitors can see
lights indicating various locations. Booking necessary.

Southwark Cathedral [3]
London Bridge, London SE1 9DAS (cathedral.southwark.anglican.org)
Large stained-glass window with depictions of Shakespeare's plays.

Museum of London [4]
150 London Wall, London EC2Y 5HN (www.museumoflondon.org.uk)
Reconstructed interiors and street scenes from the Elizabethan
period, plus contemporary articles of clothing and artefacts.

St Paul's Cathedral [5]
St Paul's Churchyard, London EC4M 8AD (www.stpauls.co.uk)
Inside is an effigy of Shakespeare's contemporary John Donne, the
only monument in the cathedral to survive the Great Fire of London
in 1666. Shakespeare's plays went on sale in the churchyard.

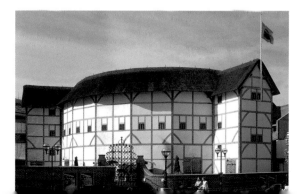

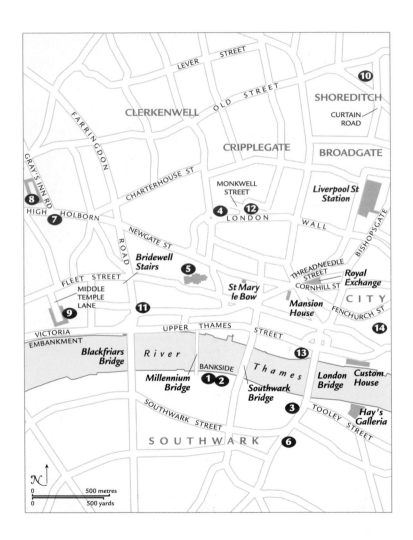

LEVER STREET

OLD STREET

SHOREDITCH ⑩

CLERKENWELL

CURTAIN
ROAD

FARRINGDON

CRIPPLEGATE

BROADGATE

CHARTERHOUSE ST

MONKWELL
STREET

Liverpool St
Station

GRAY'S INN RD

④ ⑫

BISHOPSGATE

⑧

LONDON WALL

⑦ HIGH HOLBORN

NEWGATE ST

ROAD

Bridewell
Stairs

THREADNEEDLE STREET

Royal
Exchange

⑤

St Mary
le Bow

CORNHILL ST

FLEET STREET

MIDDLE
TEMPLE
LANE

Mansion
House

FENCHURCH ST

CITY

⑪

⑨

UPPER THAMES STREET

⑭

VICTORIA
EMBANKMENT

Blackfriars
Bridge

River

⑬

Thames

London
Bridge

Custom
House

Millennium
Bridge

BANKSIDE ①②

Southwark
Bridge

③

SOUTHWARK STREET

TOOLEY STREET

Hay's
Galleria

SOUTHWARK ⑥

N

0   500 metres
0   500 yards

46

The George Inn [6]
77 Borough High Street, London SE1 1NH
No completely authentic example of a Tudor
tavern survives in the City, but the closest to it
is the George, dating from 1677.

Westminster Abbey
London SW1P 3PA
Statue of Shakespeare in Poet's Corner.

Minor Sites

Staple Inn, High Holborn [7]: Built in 1586,
this is the only half-timbered house of the Tudor
period to survive the Great Fire.

Gray's Inn, Gray's Inn Road [8]: *A Comedy of Errors* was
performed in Gray's Inn Hall in 1594.

Middle Temple Hall, Middle Temple Lane [9]: Elizabeth I
watched Shakespeare's performance of *Twelfth Night* beneath the
hall's hammerbeam ceiling in 1603.

86–90 Curtain Road, Shoreditch [10]: Two plaques
commemorate the theatre where Shakespeare first performed,
known simply as The Theatre. In 2008 archaeologists discovered
what they believe to be the footings of its foundations.

Playhouse Yard [11]: Site of the Blackfriars Theatre.

Cripplegate [12], virtually all destroyed by bombing in WWII,
lay at the junction of what is now Wood Street and St Alphage
Garden.

Old Swan Stairs, Swan Lane (near London Bridge on north
bank) **[13]**: Watermen would ferry passengers across the River
Thames from here.

St Olave's Churchyard, Hart Street **[14]**: Site of the house in
Silver Street where Shakespeare lodged with the Mountjoys.

Memorial to
Shakespeare in
Westminster Abbey

First published in the United Kingdom in 2011 by
Batsford, 10 Southcombe Street, London W14 0RA
An imprint of Anova Books Company Ltd

ISBN: 978 1 906388 93 5

A CIP catalogue record for this book is available from the British Library.

18 17 16 15 14 13 12 11
10 9 8 7 6 5 4 3 2 1

Reproduction by Rival Colour Ltd, UK
Printed by 1010 Printing Ltd, China

This book can be ordered direct from the publisher at the website
www.anovabooks.co.uk, or try your local bookshop.

Picture credits

page 1 © Russell Kord / Alamy; 2 Mary Evans Picture Library; 3 © Nigel James / Alamy;
4 (top) Map of London, from 'Civitates Orbis Terrarum', by Georg Braun (1542–1622) and Frans Hogenburg
(1635–90),c.1572, Hoefnagel, Joris (1542–1600) (after) / © Glasgow University Library, Scotland / The
Bridgeman Art Library ; (bottom) © Pictorial Press Ltd / Alamy; 5 © Mary Evans Picture Library / Alamy;
6 © Illustrated London News Ltd/Mary Evans; 7 (top) Mary Evans Picture Library/Edwin Mullan
Collection; (bottom) © The Art Archive / Alamy; 8 (left) ©Joel Newman; (top right and bottom right)
© Illustrated London News Ltd/Mary Evans; 9 © Mary Evans Picture Library / Alamy; 10 Mary Evans
Picture Library; 11 © Mary Evans Picture Library / Alamy; 12–13 © Mary Evans Picture Library / Alamy;
13 © Mary Evans Picture Library / Alamy; 14 Mary Evans Picture Library; 15 (top) Shakespeare's Globe
Image Library/John Haynes; (bottom) © Mary Evans Picture Library / Alamy; 16–17 © Classic Image /
Alamy; page 17 © Mary Evans Picture Library / Alamy; 18 © Mary Evans Picture Library / Alamy; 19 (top)
© Pictorial Press Ltd / Alamy; (bottom) © Mary Evans Picture Library / Alamy; 20 (left) © Mary Evans
Picture Library / Alamy; (bottom) Credit: Portrait said to be Christopher Marlowe (1564-93) (oil on canvas),
English School, (16th century) / Corpus Christi College, Cambridge, UK / The Bridgeman Art Library ; page
21 © Brian Seed / Alamy; 22 © North Wind Picture Archives / Alamy; 22–23 (background) © Lebrecht Music
and Arts Photo Library / Alamy; 24 Shakespeare's Globe/John Tramper; 25 © Rolf Richardson / Alamy; 26
© 19th era / Alamy; 27 (top) © World History Archive / Alamy; (bottom) © Gregory Wrona / Alamy; 28 (top)
© Jon Arnold Images Ltd / Alamy; (bottom) © Mary Evans Picture Library / Alamy; 29 (background)
© North Wind Picture Archives / Alamy; (inset) © Mary Evans Picture Library / Alamy; 30 (left) © North Wind
Picture Archives / Alamy; 31 © Geraint Lewis / Alamy; page 32 (top) Mary Evans/Interfoto; (bottom)
© Chris Batson / Alamy; 33 (top) © Mary Evans Picture Library / Alamy; (bottom) © Illustrated London
News Ltd/Mary Evans; 34 © Mary Evans Picture Library / Alamy; 35 © Lebrecht Music and Arts Photo
Library / Alamy; 36 © INTERFOTO / Alamy; 37 (top) © Mary Evans Picture Library / Alamy; (bottom)
© Mary Evans Picture Library / Alamy; 38 © North Wind Picture Archives / Alamy; 39 © North Wind
Picture Archives / Alamy; 40 Shakespeare's Globe / Ellie Kurttz; 41 © North Wind Picture Archives / Alamy;
43 © Joel Newman; 45 © ACE STOCK LIMITED / Alamy; 47 © Neil McAllister / Alamy; 48 © Jon Arnold
Images Ltd / Alamy. Map on page 46 courtesy of Martin Brown Design.